UNBROKEN
a public poetry anthology

Published by Pen & Leaf Press

penandleafpress.com

© 2025 by Public Poetry for the Authors

All rights revert to the authors on publication.

ISBN: 978-1-959743-03-3

Printed in the United States of America

This anthology presents work generated through the programs of Public Poetry, which is supported by the generous commitment of the **Houston Public Library**, the **Poetry Foundation**, the **Houston Arts Alliance**, and the **Texas Commission on the Arts**.

Preface

When Public Poetry invited writers to explore the human spirit's enduring strength, I wasn't prepared for how deeply their voices would resonate with my own understanding of what it means to remain unbroken. Public Poetry received hundreds of submissions, each carrying its own weight of survived pain and discovered grace.

As I read through the selected poems—stories of trauma and healing, displacement and belonging, despair and unexpected joy—I found myself thinking about voices that speak through us all. We carry forward not just our individual struggles, but the accumulated wisdom of those who faced their own breaking points and chose to continue.

The poets in this collection understand something essential: resilience is not about avoiding the fall or pretending the wounds don't exist. It's about the choice made in the space between breaking and rising—the decision to love and hurt, to bend without snapping, knowing that even accepting the last breath, we remain unbroken.

These seven sections mirror that journey from fracture to wholeness, but not in any neat progression. Like life itself, the path winds backward and forward, through depths and toward light, carrying all our contradictions and baggage. The voices here refuse easy comfort, demanding instead that we sit with the full complexity of what it means to endure.

In reading this anthology, I've been reminded that bearing witness is itself an act of resilience—choosing which stories resonate within us, which voices we allow to transform our understanding, which truths we carry forward. These poets have trusted Public Poetry with their most tender places. Their work stands as testimony to our shared capacity for survival and transformation.

Detrick Hughes, detrickhughes.com
Board President, Public Poetry

Table of Contents

Part I
Breaking Points

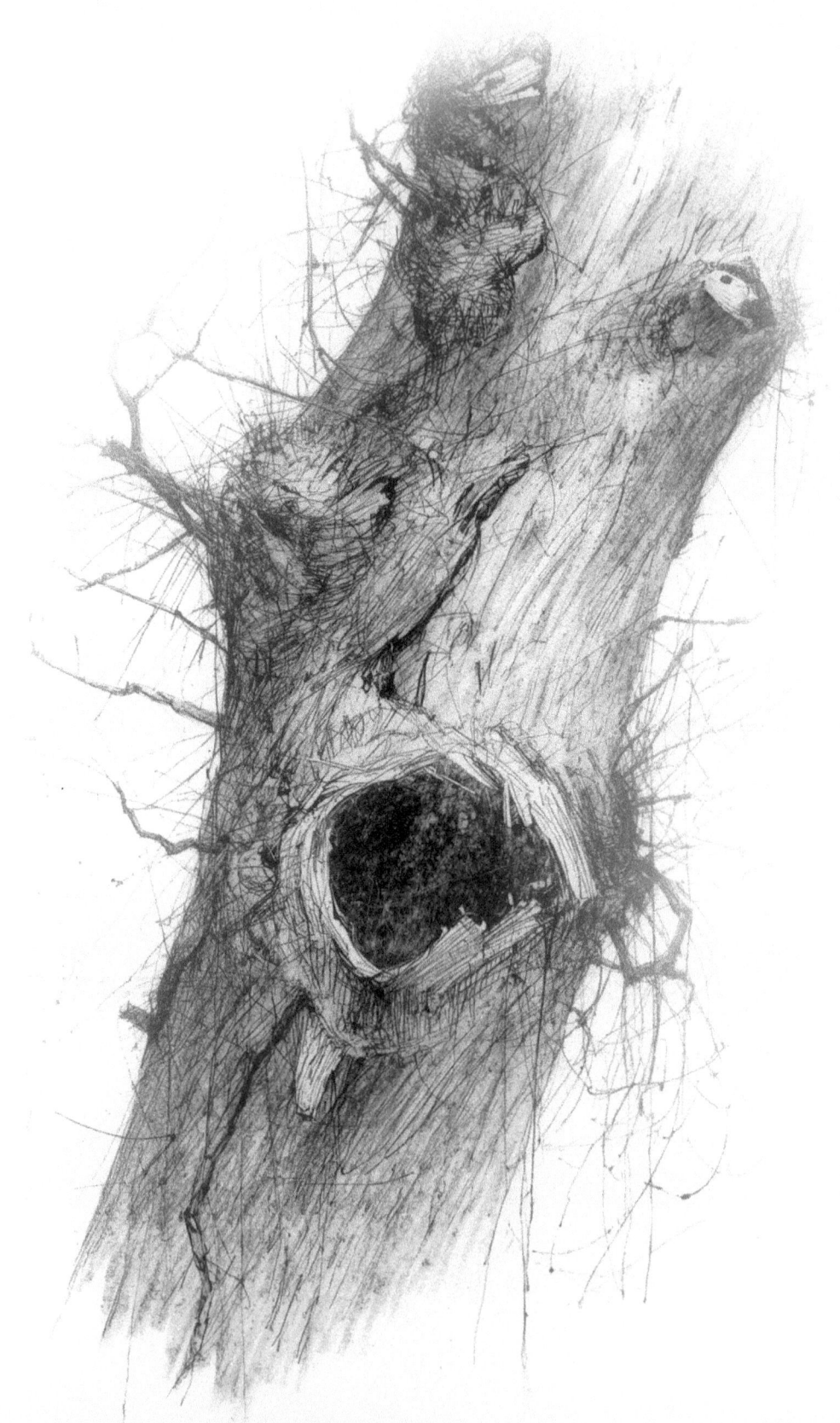

The Ghosts of Girlhood
May Garner

I am not what happened to me,
but I still carry its teeth.

My father took himself from the world
when Christmas was knocking on our door.
He left nothing but a rope, a breathless silence,
my mother screaming on our floor.

There is no easy way to soften the blow,
no way to mend that kind of wound,
no way to mute the sound of life snapping,
no matter the years that blend by.

I did not rise from the ashes; I crawled.
Fingers bloodied, knuckled ragged, knees raw,
dragging my girlhood behind me like a ghost
I wasn't ready to bury.

I became the prayer.
The storm.
Learning to hold onto grief
too large for my ribs,
too harsh for my heart,
so I made my poetry echo its pain.

There is a lick of courage
in waking up through the weight of misery
still tied to my spine,
and choosing to live anyway.

I am still here,
wearing my silence like skin.
Waiting to see if he will come back.

Some Days You Must Feel Deeply
James E Mathis

The amaryllis flower screams at me
silently, red-lipped and vulgar
while the other house plants
foreign and exotic
with wide dark hands
point their fingers at no one
listening:
how many colors do you see?

Saber, the old hound-sheep mix
her face painted in more grays and whites
than yesterday
fifteen years of pale brush strokes
asleep
dreaming of baby rabbits
and bacon and eggs
with sour-dough pancakes

My dreams are claustrophobic
office high-rise hallway nightmares
of thwarted escape
and yearning

The dog feels its bones
its muscles and sinew
the eyes blurry
but the nose reaching deeply
into the world
building a scene of scents

Far away a bean grows
on a scrub bush
in a scrub forest
on a hill touched by fog
an infant it feels
the sunshine

a prism of life-giving
knows itself

Soon a farmer moving
among the bushes
pulls berries from the branches
pauses to reflect
on the one berry
that sings color to the sun
she cries as she takes
it and places it gently
among its kin

In my multi-blue mug
handmade by a potter
crafts-woman who felt the shape
more than seeing it
and the dark brewed coffee
steam rising and swirls of liquid white
paint strokes
I see the souls there
the bush
the bean
the harvester
deep within

No Proof
Olivia Aguayo

It's kinda comical—
this body, riddled with scars
and deep cuts I cannot stitch.

It feels like my skin is dying
to show the world
I've been hurt,

told by wounds no one sees.
You can ignore the scratches from corners,
tiny cuts by random edges.

I do not care or remember
temporary discomfort.
I tell people my skin is sensitive.

But what actually causes pain
and floods these memories—
there is no visual proof.

Watch Your Step

Kelli McMullen

I am familiar with these cracks
Dividing my foundation

They are mine
And I once named them

Stubborn, Sharp
Shrewd and Bold

We watched them grow
And swallow me whole

I got to know the dark,
Desperate pieces of me

And together we decided
The relationship could not be

Smudged Edges
Collen Molahlehi

It hits you like a wave, doesn't it?
The rawness of a story
still winding and coiling like a snake.
The thick air—thicker than the blood
that has also turned its back on you.
The smudged edges,
the temptation to invite a premature ending
to this mystery still unravelling—
it tastes like defeat, doesn't it?
This elusive fate you wore when they named you,
suddenly too heavy,
too big for the shoes they once said you'd grow into.
I know they say that you shouldn't look for imperfections,
but the little cracks have grown—
taller, stronger, braver—
bold enough to show themselves
when you catch a glimpse of yourself
in the morning.
But
if I could start over,
I still don't know if I would.
Maybe it's my love for mysteries,
but I'd rather carry this regret with me
than write a perfect story.
Everyone wonders how long this story will take to pen,
but I wonder
if I'll still recognize myself
when I finally write the ending.

Manic Depression
Debra Wilk

Today
On the beach, is a day of rare but simple pleasure
Reaching for shells, my man
The one who tomorrow may be someone else
For now, this is bliss
The ease on his face, happy to be here
Not looking through me
Absent stranger
Not sitting in the car with his sour disconnect
His head full of bees under the threat of imaginary smoke
No stings today
And no clue how long
Before the dots stop connecting
The textbook pales
Bat shit crazy
Going up
Coming down
The ghost that melts into the bed for weeks
Today, he is sun and smiles, sifting sand
Saying here, take these shells, every one is a treasure
He likes my approval
I like the space in my head, the sound of the ocean
There is a stranger walking closer
Her hand extended
Here, my mother loved these
Here, please take them. Her smile fragile
I say thank you
Today, the drive home will be perfect
Today, we will stop for dinner
And he will make room for me to speak. There will be laughter
Today, will be a rose inhaled for a long grateful breath
And the bag of shells will sit on the kitchen table
Until nothing is real but his thorns
And shells, if I choose, a closer look
One is huge, shaped like a foot. One looks like a dolphin
One has a face and those special beauties Calico Scallops

Keep on loving someone's mother. Sweet stranger
Today, your name is Grace

The Addict's Mother

Anne Travers

His eyes with the speeded-up stare. You never wait for me! he screamed, coming in half an hour late for dinner. I hate you! And he threw a piece of food at me.

I told him to leave and he took his plate, walked out to his room in the garage, and left the sliding glass door to the back yard staring open.

I closed it.

He's using again. He didn't bother to deny it, just walked out the eyelid door and left it open.

Now it's morning. I've washed my face and made tea. The sun's out. It's a bright day. People are walking past.

What if he's overdosed? What if I go out there and find him lying with his eyes open like the sliding door?

If he came in last night to use the bathroom, I didn't hear him. We fell asleep after watching the basketball game. The Warriors won. Steph Curry was astonishing.

I will force this day to be normal. I will make it listen to me.

I'll do the puzzle in the paper and then go for a walk.

No. I'll wait until I've made sure he's all right. Maybe we can talk rehab. Something has to happen.

Last week, my sister in her coffin, weirdly coiffed and shrunken. And then the grave gaping open at the cemetery. Canvas covering the piled soil. The coffin teetering a little on the strong ribbons of cloth that would lower it down when we left. I leaned over to touch it and almost tumbled in myself.

The Pepsi bottle her daughter placed in the coffin for her journey, now under the earth with her in the dark.

I don't think he's going to kill himself.

I am going to shut my eyes against the possibility. I'll just sit here. I'm tired. Death is winning and I'm not Steph Curry. Often I don't even see the ball coming. I blink and I miss.

Part II
In the Depths

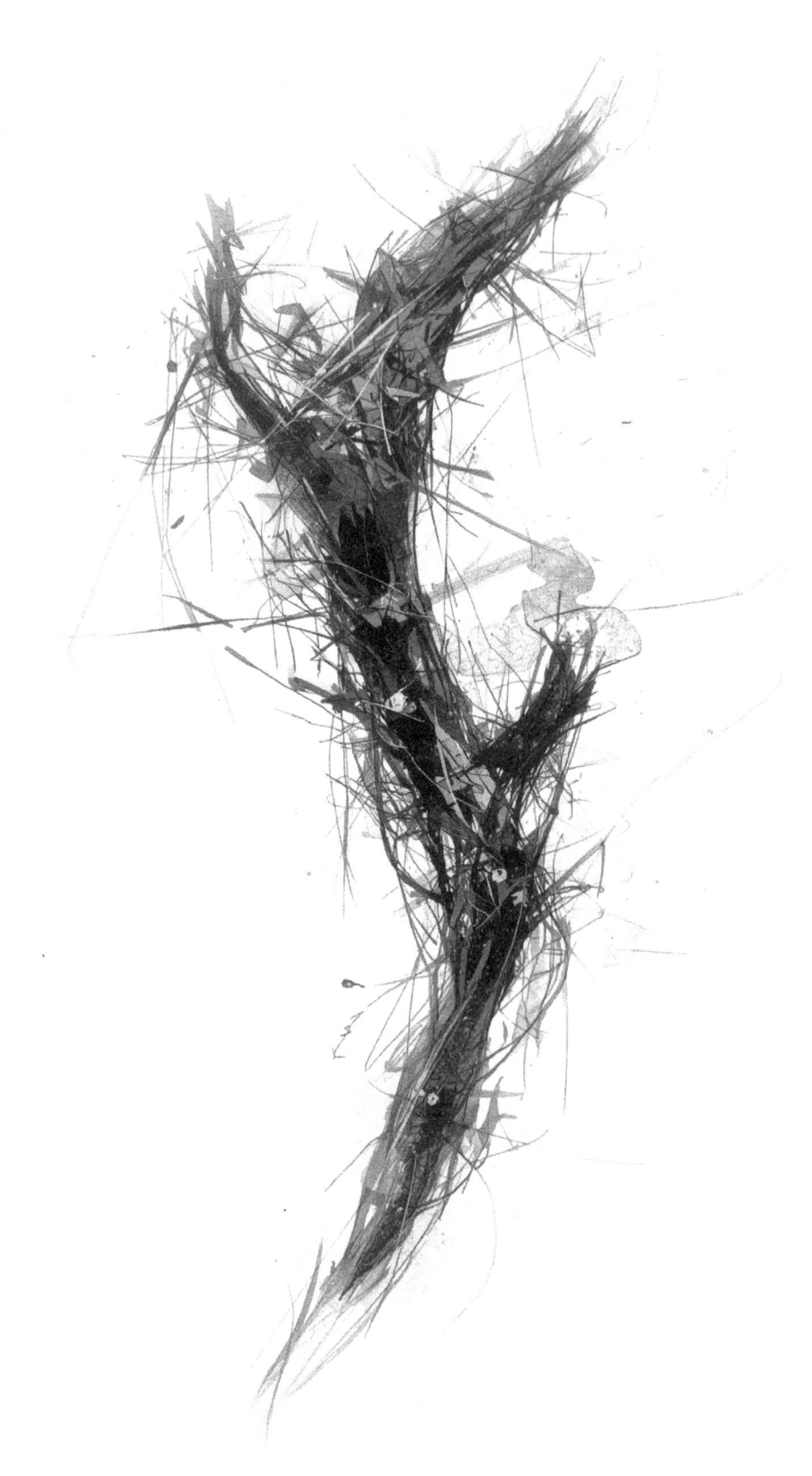

In the Year of Speechless Parliaments
Zazie Kanwar-Torge

In the year of burnt forests and speechless parliaments,
I lived in a room that dreamed of water.
Its walls seeped mildew like lost ballots;
the floorboards warped as if remembering a better script.

Most days were pale and trembled at the margins.
In the half-light, I read the news aloud to no one—
each headline a knife of forgetting,
each article a hollow tooth.

I swallowed the bitter gel-caps, the graying dawn,
learned to brew tea so dark it could stain memory.
Neighbors murmured through thin walls of layoffs,
border raids, bankruptcies,
and the clinical hush of another body gone missing in its own mind.

Yet—beneath the insomnia and its clockwork shame,
a small rehearsal of life began:
a sprig of mint forced through cracked ceramic,
a laugh escaped at the wrong moment,
a postcard from a vanished comrade slipped under the door
bearing only the words: we go on.

By summer, I grew bold enough
to pin scraps of color on the ceiling—
maps of cities unbombed,
faces unblurred,
a sun that did not flicker like a dying screen.

When they came again with their lists and orders,
I stood in the doorway unwashed but breathing,
my pulse not yet seized by the empire of no.
They asked my name;
I gave them one that had not yet been taken.

And when the moon, round and lucid as resistance itself,

rose over the scarred tenements,
I climbed the fire escape with trembling arms
and sang—
hoarse, off-key—
but whole

Appalachia
Isabella Trujillo

In swarming heaps of clouds
descending over the red canyon,
I fantasized that I broke free
from the masses and went west
searching for open prairies,
where reindeer and slick-stepped foxes reside
when they weren't hiding in hibernation.

I hoped to gaze
upon the glass door of the icy badlands
waiting long enough to witness something,
anything, that was alive,
kneeling in 20° weather
with rosy-veined pupils, foggy breath,
frostbitten with fractured knees.

The midwinter storms
creeping over ponderosa pines
and powdering snow collapsing
over and over until
the hilltop sat unbearably white
and my prayer circle had an impended interruption.

I would then conclude
my final moments awaiting
a salvation I didn't deserve.
I did hope to lay supine at peace
listening for a god that did not exist.
In my time of dying, I'd sit
cross-legged at the summit's peak
suffocated by white Tundra mist of rocky plains

to purify my lungs and fossilize my flesh
until it froze into a graveyard statue.
Onlookers would find my body
and scorn the ground I slept on—

the raven-haired Buddha in the blizzard
wiped out by a landslide.

The bystanders pretending I was never there
and fell sleep in an old black cove
where blue jays and rabbits hid from great horned owls.
Folklore would not have me poked and prodded
as the sinner in the snow
that lay with hellhound corpses

but as stupid girl with nowhere else to go
and died for nothing while being nipped at by coyotes—
raptured by vultures.

Caged in Gaza
Lynn White

She asked me why caged birds sang.
I couldn't tell her,
not for sure.
No mate will arrive this year,
and no freedom will come.
I wonder if they remember freedom,
perhaps they still
live in hope
like us.

She asked me if they felt fear as we do
when they heard the bombs falling.
I couldn't tell her,
not for sure.
I wonder if they remember peace,
Perhaps it will arrive this year,
unlike last year.
perhaps they still
live in hope
like us.

She asked me if they knew
they brought us comfort.
"I think that's why
they still sing,
like us,"
I said.

I Am Upset That Residents of Gaza Are Still Waiting for Cement to Repair Their Homes After Fear It Will Be Used for Military Purposes

John Milkereit

This cement has committed no crimes, you know?

No cement is walking like a donkey strapped with
explosives. Cement in a bag does expire.

Cement doesn't make the artillery shell
that is discourteous to someone's wall, not really,
doesn't stop a carnation blossom, doesn't seal
the border shut. Now even flowers can't be exported,
so they're just bouquets to feed sheep.

So please, let's not fear cement.

No cement wished for tunnels,
ever wanted to live in a warehouse.
This cement is a friend and should be granted
to fix one room in an apartment. What
is this wait we assign when those that suffer
can't have any cement?

People deserve better than plastic sheets for walls.

This cement doesn't ask for a happy job.
It has not been waiting to dance with its body
half-hidden near the market.

I Speak from Towers of Silence

Varsha Saraiya-Shah

It is spring, people are afraid
to sit on empty benches in parks
self-distancing. Coffin's length apart,
no matter where on the street or at work
dreading a footloose and lethal microbe.

Hugs are hats hung at the back door.
Babies like flowers can't stop being born,
mamas in hazmat suits swollen with milk
weep for their misfortune.

Imagine a massing of crows on terrace
gathered for feast to appease the dead.
Vultures plucking at corpses
I wish not to pollute air or water,
earth or fire. Let birds of prey feed on us.

Fire, Good fire, that burns to cleanse us all
of hunger and passion, anger and emptiness.
Assure the earth, it makes us part of our dirt.
Tell the skies, merge in your stardust.

O Invisible! Can you hear our dirge?
Italians belting out operas alone?
Tarantellas on balconies?
Hear the Spaniards banging pots,
strumming guitars in night skies?
Indians trumpeting conchs, chanting
Aum, Aum, Aum.

The Silence of Stones
Saba Husain

I have decided not to speak about purple
orchids on my windowsill, or the moon
in its silvery zenith, interrogating
all that the light spills on.

I will not speak, and I decided
not to, after I heard a prayer
of immense fortitude repeated
at the darkest moments
in the most desperate of times.

For years I anguished over the cries
of a kitten I could not find
the courage to comfort
because of my fears.

I will spare you the details,
because it may lead me
to question why we bother
with doves, and olive branches.

Once, I was accused of mentioning
leaves and trees in my poems,
and the morning breeze
that gives me my name, Saba,
that my grandfather chose for me.

I will be a stone, one of many
that will be called upon to speak
when the ridges of mountains disappear.

Grief
Manelle Amna Otto

Grief was more complicated than I ever thought it would be, it was a
strange thing that didn't go away.
It just moved and wriggled and morphed into different shapes that I
carried with me every single day.
For my mother it seemed to have sharpened itself into a sword.
A sword she repeatedly fell into, stabbing her deep on some days and just
scratching her on others.
I wish I could take it from her, mold it into a soft pillow she could cry
into.
But grief is a strange thing, and it doesn't go away.

Three Days

Tamara Nicholl-Smith

(In Memory of Deirdre McQuade, 1968 – 2022)

By what name do you call the whale
into whose mouth you will fall?
Into what deep ocean will you plunge
with little hope of surfacing?
Into what darkness will you wander?

The choice you have
is not the choice you would have chosen.

Will you embrace your own traitorous frame?
Its cells dividing, multiplying unbridled,
its blood carrying invasion.

The hand of affliction grips your throat.
If you cannot break free, will you
instead grab its fingers
and help them hold you, like the warrior
who when pierced, pulls the blade further inside,
the way Jesus drew his betrayer close,
broke bread and ate.

Walk into the whale's mouth,
make your home for three days
in that dark, moist maw.
Curl yourself into a ball,
hold tight and hope to last.

The choice you have
is not the choice you would have chosen:
to choose only the how
and not the 'what' or the 'if.'

This is the narrowing gate,
travel through it.
Choose that which chooses you.

Be gathered into that instance
where He said: "It is finished."

After Hospice, Weeknight, 8:00pm
Gabrielle Langley

Just before death
the mouth
falls open
into an O
an alphabet left
at the end of life.

Ammonia rises.
The stained sheets
are stripped

because aren't we always

Getting ready for the next patient

I drive home from work.
Snow and sleet
and broken branches.

My husband stirs
a pot of gumbo,
pours water,
has placed
white roses on a table.

Somewhere in the dark
he can still see
what is not death.

He knows the reverence
of silence, this hour
where human voice
would drill my ear like

fingernails on a chalkboard
this hour, every weeknight,
where I cannot speak.
Still, he hears the sounds
hiding
behind my sternum.

He will also know
that precise moment
when it's ok to tell a joke,
how to set comic relief
dead center
into a tragedy,
how to make laughter
rise like air bubbles
up to the mirrored
surface of a lake.

But in this first hour, he knows
I am swimming
I am swimming
I am swimming
upwards
through icy waters.
He knows
I will reach the surface,
will pierce black waves
like an arrow,
gasp for air,
that sharp silver inhale
where my mouth
forms an O.
This O,
it stands for oxygen.

Unseen Remains

Kelvin Johnson

As the embers surrender,
losing their last pulse of heat.

Turning from fumes yet to rise, mourning the sparks that never flared.

Glaring at ash-stained footsteps
that led to water's edge.

But the embers flare anew,
defying trembling remnants too wary to dance—
until the flames burn deep azure.

Like a frayed power line, the flame jolts slow dancing, one last time.

Ashes that never knew the blaze,
watch as flames flare, burning fierce and blue.

Like a ribbon dancer, smoke pirouettes through ruin,
grace blooming from the blaze's grave.

As the embers fade, a quiet pulse remains —
unseen by those who never cared to watch.

Part III
Mother Tongues & Other Wounds

Lupa Ng Araw
Sophia Emille

I imagine home had brown hair like mine,
with dark eyes and soft hands but a fire in her belly.
otherwise, I would not be here.
she must have beamed like guiding light—
so bright and blinding—
the way he broke in like the Word of God and
held her beneath the surface of her own waters,
until home finally stopped fighting.
come to me, he must have told her, that you may be baptized
in the name of our Lord and Savior. . .
wrestled her open upon the altar and called this a blessing.
until, of course, his blessing became her burnt offering,
and burnt offering became bastard.

this is what conquest did to our angkan:
snuffed out the sunlight of our ancestor and made bastards of us all.
how do we give thanks to a mother whose name
we do not know?
how do we tell her story when
the only part of her that survives
is the scar of seven generations of descendants
crystalized around everything she lost,
tossed to the ocean floor like pearls before swine
and a heart that was neither saved nor left behind,
only remembered in the glinting light of its broken pieces?

beloved home, know that you have not been forgotten,
that difficult, too, was our own baptism, but your bloodline survives.
I pray that every strand of this dark hair
becomes the thread that weaves me into your past life;
dark eyes, the pearls that our grandfather could not
bless into oblivion.

our grandmother, who I can only imagine had
hands as soft as the ocean breeze and a fire in her belly
so bright, it gave us the only guiding light we will ever need again.

and maybe someday we will find her name,
but until then – blessed be the name of all our ancestors,

the light that leads us home to our beloved lupa ng araw.

Sa iyong Likuran
Reymark Lubo

Ayokong hawakan ang iyong mga kamay
hangga't nabubuhay ka sa mga katha ng kahapon
Sa mga alala na pumipigil sa iyo upang umusad
at patuloy na hinahanap ang iyong sarili
mula sa kawalan na dinulot ng mga nasayang na panahon

Ngunit hindi ako magtatago
bagkus maghihintay ako sa iyo
Hanggang matagpuan mo ang kaligayahan ng puso
Kahit mahirap at masakit
Asahan mo nasa likod mo ako habang sinusubaybayan ko ang iyong
pagbangon.

Behind You (literal translation: "At Your Back")

I don't want to hold your hands
while you live in the creations of yesterday
In the memories that prevent you from moving forward
and continually searching for yourself
from the void brought by wasted time

But I will not hide
instead I will wait for you
Until you find the happiness of the heart
Even if it's difficult and painful
You can count on me being behind you while I watch over your
rise.

A Plea to the Nacirema
Collin Taylor

Mr. Medicine man, please!
I am poor, so I must beg!
My grandmother is dying, with some life left to squeeze!

This market economy has yet to offer a breeze
But my grandmother is like cattle with blackleg,
Mr. Medicine man, please!

I labor to live like the other bees
But you can pour out my dignity until there is only the coffee dreg,
My grandmother is dying, with some life left to squeeze!

I have never enjoyed a second of ease
But I would do all for her, to become a martyr or like a yegg,
Mr. Medicine man, please

Must I trade and sail across the seven seas?
Or do I kill a genius or listen to a jackleg?
My grandmother is dying, with some life left to squeeze…

…Where is the land of script and stone, please?
For I must don licorice black at that morose muskeg,
Mr. Medicine man…please,

My grandmother is dead…with no life left to squeeze

After the Revolution
Maryam Nesvaderani

Look at the photo—
an Iranian woman
in a bikini
on a beach (circa 1960)

Look at the green mountain—
feet have never touched
one grain of sand
                believe me

Look at the shopping mall—
No hijab in sight
in Paris
of the Middle East

Look—
What I am really trying to ask:
Are we
        human yet?

About Last Night
Marie Brown

About last night, a colleague and I were traveling after 10 p.m. in the heart of third ward, when we were stopped by a Houston police officer. George Floyd, Brianna Taylor, Sandra Bland, Sonya Massey's faces flashed across the windshield of the car, holding their hands up while their bodies swayed from side to side. The officer asked for my driver's license and registration. My colleague immediately reached in the compartment and retrieved the registration along with other items like candy wrappers, grocery receipts, and sticky notes to self. I saw Philando Castile face looking at me from the passenger's side window. I asked the officer, "why did you stop me"? I quickly thought, maybe I should not have asked that question. I fumbled through my purse finding everything but my driver's license, my Texas Southern University I.D., my library card, photos of my grandchildren wondering if I will live to see them again, wondering if one wrong move and I will no longer grace this earth, and one day haunt as a shadow across someone else's windshield. The officer said, "your front headlight is out on the driver's side, see come look". My colleague and I both looked at each other, I saw an image of Walter Scott running. We replied, " Nah that's okay we will stay in the car". The officer was polite and respectful; however, we should not have to feel this way, at all, at any time at any place. "If we do not tell our stories, we will fuel the fire that will burn us alive".

Time-lapse
Katelyn Brown

All Great cities sink, I think.

The cities that carry the title great and remain, must not be all that
fantastic. For its secrets to be shared, quite wildly -- like the special show
from a wandering circus -- amongst its patrons recounting exclusive,
lavish, and marvelous events of misplaced memories. Continuously citing
'you just had to witness it at that moment'.

Secrets shared between foreigners -- excluding the consideration of a
native to correct, counter, or clarify their misguided conclusions of the
limitless myth to greatness. To misshape and redirect the historic melody
of time that the body, people, and land before them truly display.

And when an ill-advised, torturous, and unwieldy soul makes it a mission
to seek out all the glorious stories that have been recounted -- regrettably,
meagerly -- as a means for a deeper connection to the world around them
-- to comprehend humanity, they will find the opposite of what was
sought; disenchantment (not clarity). The unfounded profession of Great.

But I suppose that's the point. Great cities are not meant to last,
uninterrupted, for centuries. They are meant to be experienced
momentarily, similar to countless, pleasurable, human affairs.

And so, Houston sinks. With time of course. In addition to a changing
climate. Across multitudes.

I think all Great cities sink, especially when their touring patrons
recognize the brilliance of its essence. Making the continuous claims of
'you just had to be there'..

It's a meticulously cultivated process.

Part IV
Transformation

The Kintsugi Butterfly
Gabrielle Vasquez

Oh, dinky Mapwing butterfly,
Fluttering through the black-thorn rose bushes,
Your wings tattered and frayed—
How beautifully your dried blood stains.

How courageous you are after all these arduous years,
Watering roses with your silent tears.
In the sublime gardens where you reside,
Have you ever glimpsed what waits on the other side?

Mapwing butterfly, never be dismayed by your name,
For a single ivory floribunda rose awaits.
With its healing petals that never wilt, soft as silk,
Allow yourself to be rebuilt.

And watch how the cracks you once hid in shame
Transform into that which earns most acclaim.
The scars on your back will transmute to gold,
And legends of the kintsugi butterfly will be told.

Equilibrium

Jennifer Villegas

I live in the tremble
between lightning and thunder—
that breathless hush
where epiphanies taste like copper
and madness hums a lullaby.

Not saint, not fool,
but the hinge on which both swing,
watching galaxies spin
from the corner of my eye
while my coffee grows cold.

The mystics call it grace.
The doctors call it a symptom.
I call it Tuesday.

I've walked the knife-edge
of too much clarity—
where even shadows have shadows
and silence screams in perfect pitch.

I'd rather be half-ghost
than choose a side.
Let the philosophers argue;
I'll be planting dandelions
in the cracks of their cathedrals,
laughing when the wind
scatters all their certainties.

Some say balance.
I say: "Dance in the avalanche."
The edge is the only place
wide enough to breathe.

Dreams
Roshni Baig

Joyously, the wind sighs
As I sit by the lake
watching trees reflect
between waves

Happy, yet I keep
sad lines
of my Urdu poem
tucked away

Childhood friends
circle me—
ones I wished to meet—
in full color,

life rushing back
in fragments of joy,
sorrow,
loss, success rebuilt

I escape—weave
these fragments into a tapestry
of desires and people
loved and hated

When I wake-- reality
offers challenges, ignites
courage where nightmares
vanish with the waves

Haiku - the path
Lucy Lunt

Concrete pavers
lead to the compost heap
Tiny snakes hide inside

early road (an aubade)
Curtis L Crisler

in this aubade, day reaches over
night—a blanket of muted light,
lightly splashing your eyes from

an angel's breath, fluttering your
dark lashes to open to rude day—
a releasing of night's cuddle—

unlocking, like unclenching the
toddler's grasp of your t-shirt, how
careful they are to keep you close.
~
starlings do thick murmuration
over interstate bridge. birds can
crash you into reality in lil bursts.

there are houses off the interstate
where i just need to knock on red
doors for entrance. but, i never do.
~
i woke up at 5am to deliver a poem
to a room full of people—2 hours
there, 2 hours back, in this open

world, sliding from dark to light—
some slight-of-hand. but there is no
illusion to the dedication of breathing.
~
right now, i don't like your food.
i don't like your music. i don't like
your women. they have too much

salt in them. preserved like sweaty
hopes—dangling like smoked fish
campers store out of the reach of bears.

~

i never dreamed of voices screaming
my name in crowds—my face on
statues and paintings. i never wanted

anything but to breathe along with
you—one breath. one heart. one
reaching for your every and anything.

Present Danger (A Reverse Poem)

Pallavi Kapilavaih

The past is the only break I am promised
I do not insist
I shall walk under a sky that does not open as if it may
In this sun-drenched town - the rain I chase falls in a place not far away
Yesterday and yesterday and yesterday
Behind
Is the only direction to which my eyes are inclined
Ahead
The same, same disdained onward sped
I can bear no more
Of this turning - undoing return my amber shore
What is hope but the origin
For a gambler's addiction
I have no proclivity
Towards Spring's mythology
The poppies bloom having forgotten desert summers
And rooting where nothing but dust remembers
My sunlit roses – green thorned only from envy
I will never be
Free from sands that always give less than they take
The future is a promise I will break

Part V
Despite Everything, This

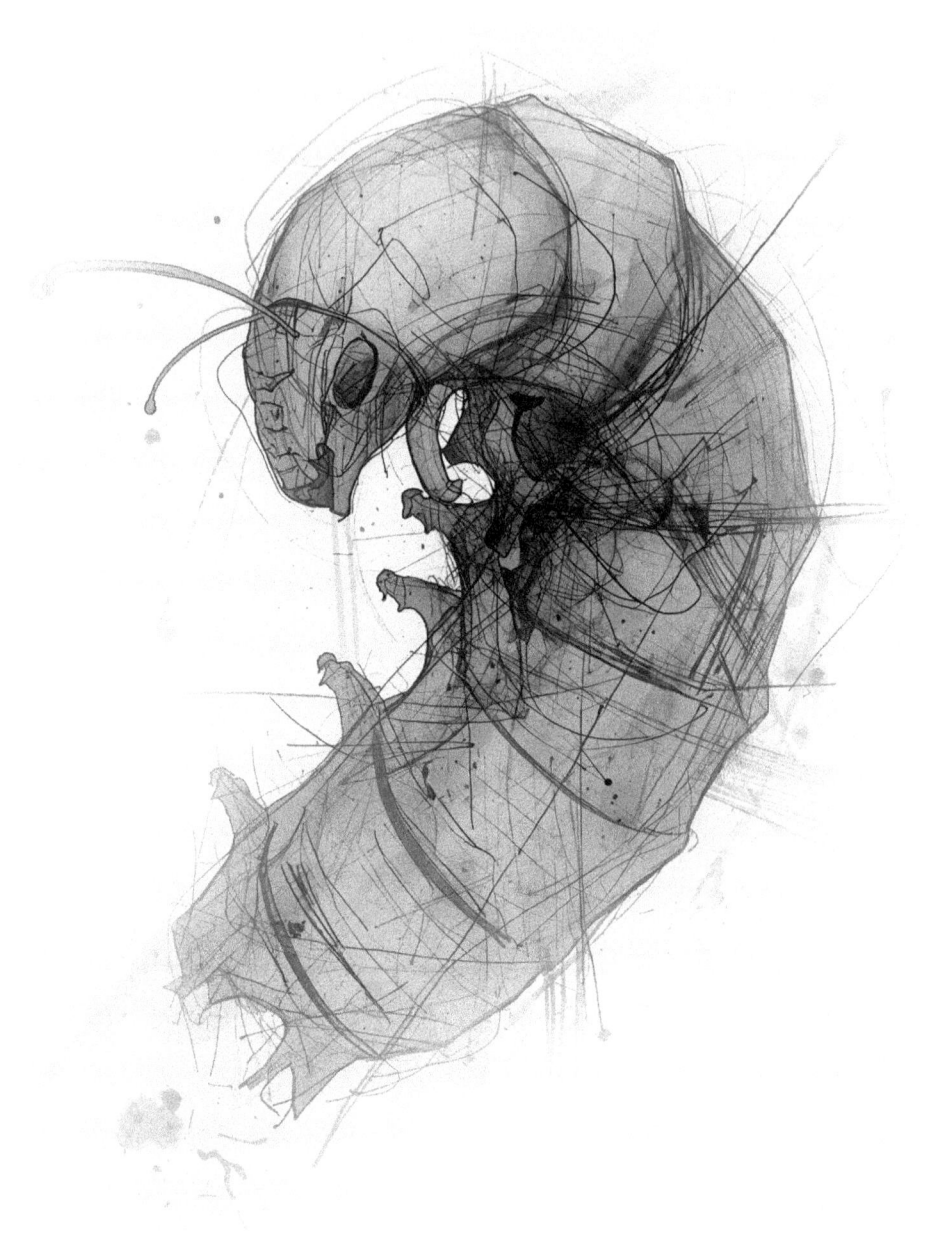

The Best Sex of Our Lives

Patricia Campagna

We had the best sex of our lives today.
I am 58. He is 72.
We thought we couldn't beat Suite Prado
in Madrid, summer of 2013,
but we did. We did it today.
The world collapses outside.
America implodes.
Markets wither, science gasps.
Firms weather fierce squalls,
Colleges slide into sink holes.
And here we are,
breaking our own record for kicks.
There are still delights to be had
on any given day.

The One Who Shares My Moon

Bhumi Raghav

You, moon, are never far—
you linger in the pauses I breathe when no one's watching.
I speak to you in murmurs,
when the earth is asleep and my heart wide awake.
And you listen, I know—
I feel you gently holding my feelings in the folds of your light.
You move with my moods,
my quiet reflections cast through the window,
in patterns only we can read.

And maybe that's how one carries love, isn't it?
The way the world sees scars,
but we see stories.
Isn't that what love truly is—
finding beauty in what others call broken?
Maybe the truth is,
we don't fall in love despite the cracks,
but because of them.
These are stories, I believe—
not imperfections,
but the signature of who we are.

Sometimes, I wonder—
as this quiet warmth blooms inside me
just by watching you move,
just by admiring your presence—
what if I'm not the only one feeling this?
What if that warmth is shared?
What if it's his warmth, reaching me somehow?

Somewhere beneath the same silver pearl,
he might be looking at you too,
unaware that you're carrying pieces of us,
as you always have.

I dream that someday,

under the same sky,
you will be the witness to our union—
as you've always been
to our quiet, unspoken longings.

You have always been mine,
and soon,
you will be ours.

Comorbidly Yours
Leticia Urieta

For my disabled loves

You don't ask, "have you tried...?"
We know better

Instead, dump your bag out on the table
out spills
hand sanitizer
face masks in a rainbow array
a HEPA filter, a beacon of purple UV light
hand warmers for this chilly day
nasal sprays ("take one, I have extra")
oils for calming
oils for dry skin
oils for the joints
a magical exchange of remedies from
the whisper network in the land of the ill

Medical blue gloved hands come disembodied
from a room that won't meet your eyes
but wants you to slip that mask down
just to see your grimace

Care comes from the hands of beloved
coconspirators bringing tea to the table
Being outside with you, sweating or chilled
is a miracle
you always send me on my way
with gifts
stickers you made yourself
a handful of figs from your yard
bluebonnets to plant early and wait
We won't see them grow for another year
or two
but everything planted takes root
breathing hard under hot packed earth

54

* * *

life happens here
the whispers that grow louder
each time we press our smiles
against each other's heart windows
they're reserved, conserved, for those who can
feel them even behind the mask

Carline Playlist

Courtney O'Banion Smith

Love, love is a verb.
Love is a doing word.
Elizabeth Fraser, Massive Attack

We sit within the adrenalized heartbeat-
rhythm of our carline playlist:
repetitive bass, strings plucked at the speed
of sound, and brain-soothing
beta waves roll over us as we wait.
He's always been good
with patterns. Are you sure
you don't want to take up drums
again?

I point out when one layer of sound
fades and another crescendos,
overtakes it, try to explain
DJs and mixing, confusing his obsession
with rhythm video games and pacing
in his bedroom to techno on loop
with a potential passion I should
encourage for a future career.

I just want to listen, okay, Mama?

I go quiet, bob my head
to the tamer-than-usual electronica.
Ambient EDM vibrates through
the pearlescent doors of the vehicle,
our tense bodies. Taillights blink
on and off as we stop and go.
I remember dance clubs,
mix tapes. I swipe to unlock,
tap the repeat icon.

Enveloped in notes,

I glance in the rearview.
Lost in sound, his translucent face
reflected in the window
looks back at him.

Knowing pressure kills joy,
I don't repeat what a good singer
he could be, instantly worry
I'm letting him down
by letting him off. The music swells,
turns. He sees me looking. Smiles.

What?

The car inches forward.

Suspended in waves,
we float together,
the listening enough.

Cabaret
Lee Anthony Molano

You're pretty in low dim light
My mind filling in the blanks of your features
Pretending you're someone you're not.
A warm body at the least, odd considering your skin is cold.
Here in a place I told myself to forget
Finding myself in your gaze, lost in a grip again.
Sex comes and goes
Yeah we all come and go.
You can come and go.
I think tonight I'd rather just be alone.
At least at this moment distract me from myself,
And give me something to reflect on when I'm feeling a new low.

Part VI
Resilience & Renewal

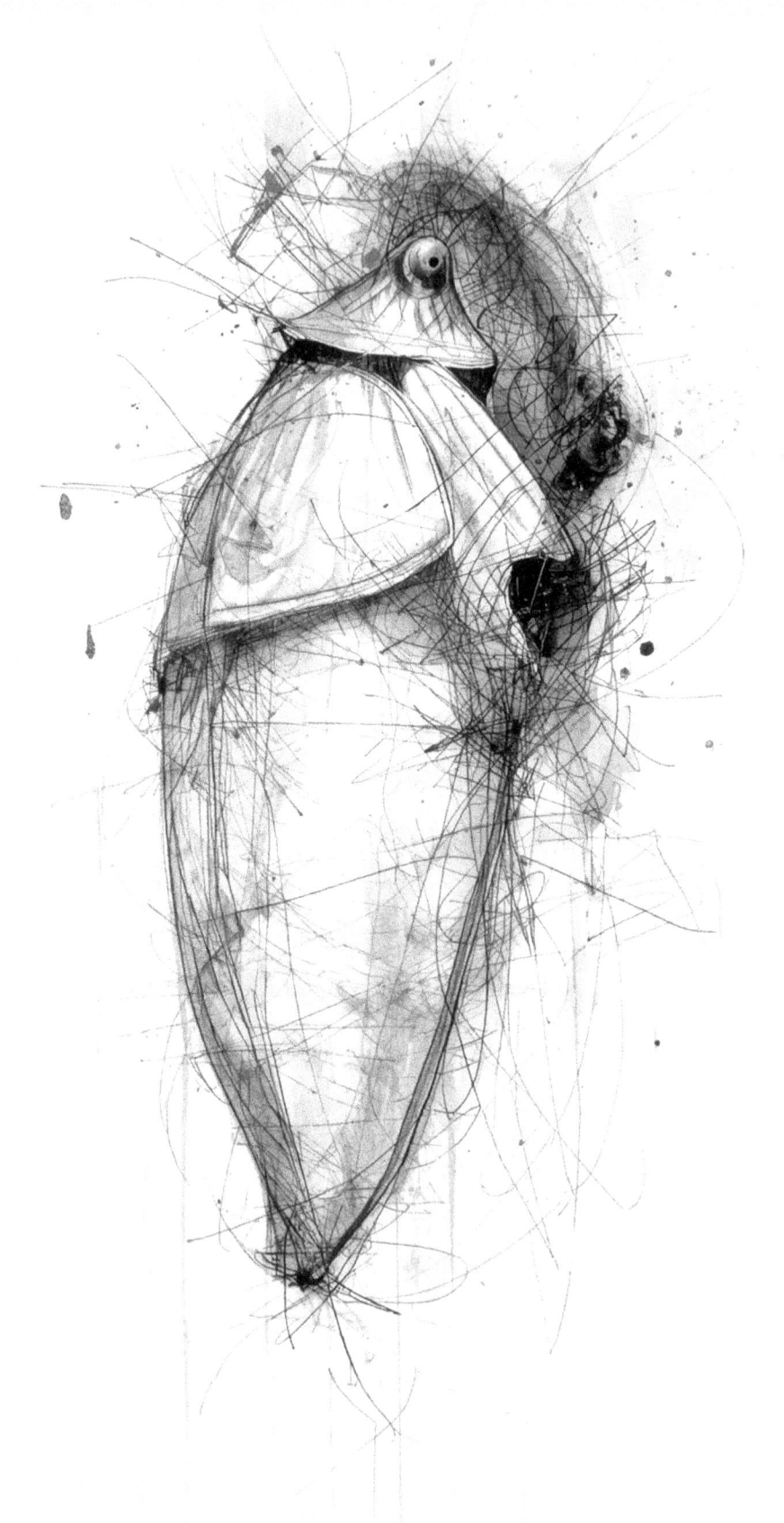

Because
Elizabeth S Wolf

Because I survived
I must speak out;
Because I survived
I must blend to pass.

Because I have endured
months in your wards and
hours crawling the floors of welfare offices,
stared through plate glass windows of restaurants
hungering in the streets,
I have seen the naked bones
of society's fortress.

Because I have emerged, risen from ashes
earned degrees by day, working
flat on my back through long groping nights,
have learned to walk and talk and
dress like you, to carry credit cards
and expense receipts,
I must blind myself to my past.

Because I have been scarred
I must be a revolutionary.

Because I have defied narrow expectations
I burn bright with the power of joy.

Because a beacon shows others the way
to be light: to dare, not only to beam dreams

but to fight to make them come true.

Do not Call us Broken

Terry Egharevba

Failure visits us
but we make her sit at our table,
feed her stories of our ancestors—
warriors who wrestle storms barehanded,
midwives who birth hope in famine—
until she grows weary of returning.

We are the architects of endurance,
the clay reforged by flame,
the unbroken thread
pulling generations upward.

We fall, yes
but never break.
Our bones weld to history's spine,
our flesh stitches itself
with the same sinew
that holds our forebears upright.

Here, where dawn wears the face of a test,
we rise—
hammering light from darkness,
kneading miracles from dust,
our sweat the mortar,
our prayers the stone.

With nothing but hands
that shape absence into abundance
we push tides beyond their reach,
read maps in scars,
dream through nights armored in lack.

We are the tremor beneath rubble,
the hammer that outlives its handle,
the living decree—
We Do Not Break.

* * *

Call us liars
our scars will laugh.
Whisper "broken"
and watch our ancestors
rise in our bones.

Survived
Caroline Ross

If I could call you, I would boast about it.
You would say, "well done!"
Also, was the worst thing you have ever
Done to me,
(dying, I mean)

Expecting that I would be
Expected to be
Just fine about it
- Well, I was not - and
Three hundred and seventy days later
When I rose from an unspeakable grief
That still didn't kill me -

I realized I had even hated you for a while
For not being here to apologize outright for
not being immortal
And leaving me here
Without you.

I knew also that you understood this
Because you always understood everything

I just want you to know that I
Survived.

A Kitchen of My Own
Aishwarya Balasubramanian

My wish is to have a kitchen of my own, where violence has no home

Where dishes can slip from my hand and my body doesn't freeze

Where I can make mistakes and don't have to move to the other corner

So I am not anyone's obstacle to cross, because I am slow to the general population

Where I can take my time to admire the smell of my coffee, the sun, the passing of time

Without needing to rush or quickly leave due to an impending fight taking shape in the background

A kitchen of my own where violence has no home

Where things can slip from my hand Where I don't have to shut my ears in default response

A kitchen I choose to cherish, with colours, softness, tenderness of love and nostalgia

A kitchen I can share with a loved one with whom we will build new love stories together

A loved one with whom we will navigate our demons together, hug each other's wounds without the stamp of conditions and fickle attachments

A kitchen of my own, which will feel like home

With space, with air to breathe and cook at my own pace

Music ringing in the background not as an escape

A kitchen of my own with no banging of utensils, with no explosion of voices

Where the space is a melody, not a dissonance

A kitchen where peace truly stays
A kitchen not marked by eggshells
A kitchen that is not a battleground

A kitchen where love is the song and care is the tune
A kitchen where affection is proudly displayed

A kitchen where food is made and eaten together as a happy family

A kitchen of my own from where I don't have to run away

A kitchen of my own, one which I can finally call my home

Done
Charlene Stegman Moskal

I believe I'm done
improving myself;
come as far as I want to,
just want to stop and smell the roses
not contemplate the life of bees.

I believe I'm done
with coming and going,
time in, time out; it's all the same.
The more you know
the less you care
or the less you know
or something like that.

I believe I'm done
with theories of existence,
the multiverse,
rhythms of reality,
deep breathing exercises
whose goal is to get you
in touch with yourself.

In the words of someone wise:
Who the fuck else
would I be in touch with?

I believe I'm done
with chair yoga,
strength stretching,
books on self-awareness
and mindfulness,
contemplating unity in nature,
the paisley patterns of all things

I believe I'm done with the assumption
I'm broken, need to be fixed.

I am not broken, only old.
The blood of generations
of strong women moves through me.
It's the spirit that counts.
So, believe me when I say back off,
I am anything but broken.

The Women Inside Me
Jael Uribe

Me,
and all the women inside me
all the ships burning in my eyes
all the harbors without shores...
There are women who never stop at the edge.
They turn hunger into continents,
weave their grandmothers voices into a song,
and shift the wind direction.

Many die in my womb,
in the sleeping echo
though no one sleeps
in the illusory things
no one dares to dream.
Me, and the crack in the drums.
Me, and the scar in time
that echoes slowly
in empty houses and stray dogs.
Women know the weight of the earth.
Even the moon surrenders
to those who dare
to face her directly.
I am not silence—
I am the scream that tears open,
roots that cling
to the ground others feared to tread.
Me, who has learned to dance
with the ghosts of fear,
carrying in my steps the memory of all who fell,
and in my chest,
the rhythm of resistance.
I am the poem no one dared to write,
but have always existed,
waiting for the voice of a woman
to be brave, to be born, to have strength to rise.

My Little Things Are Big Things
Marium Ayub

He told me if I get excited over
"Every little thing" then I'll
miss out on the 'Big' things.

The achievements worthy
of being celebrated, you know
the really Big things.

How was I to explain to him that,
after not wanting to live for so long–
trapped, suffocated, depressed.

The only way I could hold on
for dear life, were the little things.

The way sunshine illuminates
the night's dark & gloom.
For it knew and it knows,
of the warmth it brings into
spaces and into my heart.

The days when I have no energy,
to move, to think, to feel or to exist,
sunshine filters into my room,
inching closer & closer
to my motionless body.

Kissing my toes first, letting the
warmth of its touch soak into my skin.
Moving upwards still,
till it washes all over me
in its kind & loving embrace;
whispering to my soul,
'Another day has come',
'You've survived another one'.

Her tender warmth comforting me.
With it, the birds awaken,
ready to start another day.
Their tweets, coo's & chirps
coaxing me out of bed.

Their songs stirring something within,
shattering through the numbness
I have felt for so long;
whilst the sun's rays seduce me,
with the promise of a new day.

Perhaps, I will survive it too.
And with each day, I have.

How, then, could I describe to him,
my sweet solar seductress & her bird songs,
when he refused to appreciate my existence
& thus, also, the little things that have
sustained my soul for so long.

Part VII
Finding Light

I Do Not Have to be Good
Margaret R Sáraco

What if I were to remove myself
from the demands of the world?
Love what I love, take what I need
Nourish my body with care
Allow my mind to wander
Like on a hike in the woods
Waiting for bird calls
As animals scurry by
Inside the forest
Past the whisper of trees
That space found inside
Without going anywhere.
The forest is a good place to be
on a crisp, fall morning.
My mind could be those trees
Welcoming others along the path
I could be that
I could be there.

What if we were to remove ourselves
from the demands of the world?
Love what we love, take what we need
Nourish our bodies with care
Allow our minds to wander
Like on a hike in the woods
Lost in thought
Waiting for the sound of birds
As animals scurry by
Inside the meditation of the forest
Past the whisper of trees speaking
That place, that space found inside
Without going anywhere.
The forest is a good place to be
on a crisp, fall morning
Our minds could be trees
Welcoming one another along the path

* * *

I could be that
You could be there with me.

Freedom
Lind Grant-Oyeye

Is the word on the street —
Not my street,
Not yours,
Not the man's crawling through
Whatever remnant was left
Behind the tree that carries stigma,
Like the tattoo on wild backs —
The way it marks everything except
The ink marks it.
Freedom is the word in the alley,
The one we embrace,
Running toward someplace:
Someplace healing,
Someplace sealing,
The hope — like liquid —
Sticking hard bark
To a broken tree.

The Hero

Sandi Stromberg

I'm driving I-45 in Houston,
where I've been
abandoned, but a job is a job,
and I'm a single parent.
Though my eyes won't focus,
I keep my foot pressed
to the floor like a Formula 1
driver. Morning rush-hour
is unforgiving. It's a long road
when you face the world alone,
Mariah Carey sings. I belt out,
"Don't I know it!" I'm finally learning
heartache isn't just an expression.
It's a bodily condition, a wound
pulsing with each beat,
like a finger digging into a bruise.
And just like that, everyone knows
the marriage wasn't a fairy tale,
he was no Prince Charming,
and playing Cinderella didn't prove
my foot fit the glass slipper, yet he's still
the hero, his therapist says—
for saving himself. There may be
no fairy godmother, but
I'm a dove risen from the stone.
I'm the double rainbow
arched over the freeway ahead.
I'm the Queen of Swords,
blade poised at the knot.

State of Grace
Robin Reagler

Nobody lit the fire. A luminous arrow
split the cloud into parts. A braided pony
glanced away. A lake reflected the flames
until they were spent. Feeling your way
through a forest maze, you are finding
an opening where none ever existed before
today. Your watch died hours ago. In an imaginary
cottage, yes, a kettle of pecans basting in hot
cooked sugar. A woman stirring the pot.
When a compliment comes out of your mouth,
a moth flies in. The trick is in remembering
every detail, what happened next. And why.

¿Cómo amaneciste?
Sandra Gustin

I dawned like a blanket of roseate spoonbills over mangroves of the Magdalena.

I dawned like civilization, maybe the World Trade Center or the Tower of Babel.

I dawned like an idea bursting through gray matter, synapsing down to dark muscles.

I dawned like a masterpiece yet to dry, probably a Van Gogh.

I dawned like the skirt of a woman dancing cumbia, flicking first forward, then back.

I dawned like a sailor at sea, eyes weighing the red sky.

I dawned like the Golden Gate Bridge, bolstered on fog.

I dawned like Pablo Escobar's invasive hippos, wreaking havoc on waterway and farms.

I dawned like an elder daughter rising from a vigil over her father's hospital bed.

I dawned like a housewife who left the dishes the night before.

I dawned like an insomniac, early enough to sit with the Morning Star.

It was raining, but I dawned like an arepa con huevo, sun and energy inside.

Redemption
Hiba Rasheed

My father's grave
My father's 17 year old grave
And I went to visit him only yesterday
After a decade of silent prayers
Tears raging, holding fists at me, for having been finally set free,
Not for a sad movie ending or weight loss frustration
But for a worthy cause fulfilling their ultimate purpose of soul
     purification

Mental lacerations burned as flashbacks of his sage
     sayings flashed through like
Love is the essence of life or
White is in the heart, not in the skin
When white kids ridiculed my dark skin
My dark skin, one of my bonds to him

For months, I have been trapped inside my lackadaisical thoughts
     and lackluster vision of hope
While electric shocks, emitting toxic waste, coursed through my head
Contaminating my veins
So I became a walking wasteland of shriveled dreams and shelved faith
But somehow, somehow
In my barren state
My father beckoned to me
After a decade of silent prayers
Water gushed forth through the pores of my desolation
Flooding my senses
Like Zamzam's[1] answer to Hajer's[2] desperation
On the holy ground
I then heard the muffled sounds of chains breaking
     under the wrath of waves
And I remembered

* * *

---

[1] Muslim Holy Water
[2] Prophet Abraham's Wife

I remembered
His unwavering smile throughout the long nights,
coming home late, 3 jobs, burying his exhaustion
under his sleeves to cook us dinner willingly and lovingly
I remembered
His unwavering smile through his tears of joy at our smiles of joy
The "never look up but at less fortunate people
	so you can be grateful for your blessings,"
The encouragement to be the best that I can
His diabetes, multiple heart attacks
And that last heart failure,
	that last heart failure which ended his life too soon on an ordinary
Thursday night, after dropping us off at the park, young and free,
	promising to pick us up later
but never made it

Baba danced with the wolves around that bonfire
	called life through kindness, humility, love and
that warm, embracing, never-failing smile
Unleashed this cannonball of retrospection
To remind me that the goodness which was in him is in me too

6 feet deep
Withered remains
Yet his heart still beats in mine

Flowers Never Picked

Cody Draco

I used to want you to pick me
out of a field of a thousand flowers
but you never did and I am grateful
that I am still attached to my roots
that my stem remains unbroken
by harsh hands that were glazed
with a modest tan
once a flower is picked
it is most often placed in a vase
given water and a gaze
for a limited number of days
eventually wilting out of shape
the beauty of flowers never picked
is that they will bloom again
and again
and again

Flawed
MG McMullen

Amid the electrons
in their atoms
the cells
move about in the dark
with only an internal light
to guide them
they move and produce energy
in the perfectly ordered structure
of their synchronized machine

But something went wrong with me
somewhere there is a dead spot
nothing moves
no light
no energy is produced
I am the antithesis of order
I am chaos
the creator forgot me
and left this small space, my space,
void, a nothingness
like the universe
before he spoke his word

This void cries out
to be filled
and ordered
with energy
with light
it is the secret I keep
my thorn
a glitch in the engine

He touches it with his finger
"Not dead," he says
"just broken"
How does he do that

I wonder?
I see it emanate light
a different light
not bright white
like the rest
but glowing and blue
it moves
but moves
in a different direction
counter clockwise

"Are you sure the engine can run?"
I ask
"Yes," he says
"Are you sure?"
"Trust"
A strange gift
a gag gift
it makes me laugh
we laugh together
this is the essence of gift
this is grace

Listening to Lou Reed Sing "I Heard Her Call My Name" With Moe Tucker on the Drums
Kathi Crawford

Who was the dead girl he heard calling him
out of the Velvet Underground?
Standing above the bass drum
upside down on the floor,
banging tambourines with mallets,
Moe split my listener's mind.

Early drums were made of hollowed
tree trunks, alligator skin stretched across,
struck with hands.
In sixth grade, my mom gave my drums
to my brother. She said,
"You can't play them because you're a girl."
That fateful forking over
of my drum kit left me
striking my wood tips on pots and pans
instead of the snare.

I am the dead girl now.

Music notes as shadows
lead me back like a conductor.
How could I give up my dream
to play in a rock and roll band?

It's not impossible to find your rhythm.
It's never too late to pick up the sticks.

When you're dead,
no one can kill you. Don't say—
you can't live the life of your dreams.

Desideratum[1]
Karen Rigby

I rinse apricots, trace the crease
in their buttery skins.

Milk-yellow, blush, fiery gifts.
Each fruit an envelope

wrapped around its stone.
I rub the scent of Royal

on my thumbs. Slice fruit
into quarter-moons, soak flesh

in rum cool from the cellar.
All winter I dreamt of lifting

the bottle I'd tucked between
two rafters, of shattering

glass. Now, the voyage.
I hand you a bowl

lined with festival boats.
Not one bruise. God love you

if these are not enough.

---

[1] Desideratum was previously published in Festival Bone (Adastra Press, 2004)

Workaround

Judith Oppenheim

I sip hot rum by the hearth,
Where burnished white coals grovel, gleam.
Nod off to a dance in the badlands.
Bodies tremble, hands clap,
Faces blink on a tiny screen.

Features bleed like paint that ran.
My ears hear noise,
My brain reads sand.
Sand that empties through the pinch
Of a waisted glass.

Pitching precious grains one-at-a-time,
My dear, deaf, ASL friends
Pull their PIN's in quick succession
Hurled from swirling gestures,
So-sharpened word clouds gather.

Also known as conversation,
These high impact projectiles hit
On message, fully punctuated,
With eye contact, a full-brain/body workout,
No batteries, no two-factor verification.

Stringing Beads while Singing along to Stevie Nicks' Gold Dust Woman Not Caring Who Hears Me Now
Maria Merrill

How many life events does a woman need to live
to claim she's living fully? I string crystals
from my grandmother's chandelier
on thick ochre cord, a necklace for a giant.
Don't say you haven't noticed.
My mom's necklace of turquoise beads
hangs in my bathroom hallway.
You enjoy the contrast of the pale blue color
on the blood red wall. I don't think to wear it.
Myself and other students in our yoga-trauma
class link up like beads in twine. We sit in a half circle
holding each other together so we won't fall apart.
I used to wear a gold chain with a lotus flower
charm around my neck. I would sleep, shower,
fuck, live in it. I only took it off when the gold
turned silver. I'm not sure you noticed.
Later I bought a "wish" necklace, made a wish, tied it
around my neck. The string didn't break
over months of 24-hour wear. I cut myself free.
The wish un-granted. I didn't care.
Did you know I once had a lover
who wore a jaguar tooth on a chain? It was vulgar
and attention grabbing. Cut off my breath.
A necklace that could hurt, like he did me.
I wish I had giant rocky rubies, citrines,
sizzling colors, to give my smallest students,
instead of beige-pink and yellow-beige stones.
Scavenging as a sport no longer excites me. My friends
and I sit around the table drawing our desires
for the year ahead. A necklace of words,
a torn collage. I notice my body melting.
It's no longer hard for me to make something
beautiful from something discarded. I'm the last
kid in a candy shop, hands in every drawer
topaz, tourmaline, emeralds overflowing.

Indestructible Poem
Alexis Krasilovsky

Here is a poem
designed to withstand anything.

What are a few tears
on a sullen ocean

or snowflakes
on a melting glacier?

Will this poem
disappear
on line

like a thrashing fish,

or if I try
reading it out loud

will it get caught
like glass splinters
in my throat?

About Public Poetry

Launched in 2011, Public Poetry has created collaborative programs and projects in the City of Houston. Thanks to generous donors and grantors, we are able to present poets, filmmakers, and artists through various partnerships with local libraries, music venues, theaters, colleges, and universities. Our programs include a monthly reading series with the Houston Public Library, our annual anthology publication, LOCATION | HOUSTON, and more. To learn more about our nonprofit and support our work, please visit our website at publicpoetry.org and follow us on social media.

About the Contributors

Bella Trujillo is a Colombian American writer and poet from Houston, Texas, currently studying Creative Writing at the University of Houston.

Cody Draco is an emerging queer poet, settled but never stagnant, creatively restless in the rural sanctuary of southern Kentucky.

Collen Molahlehi is a poet and engineering student in Johannesburg, South Africa. His poetry centers on love, grief, and mental health. Published in anthologies in South Africa, the USA, and the UK, he won first prize in the AVBOB Mini-Poetry Competition in 2025. Instagram: @Just_Collen

CJ Mathis's work appears in Brilliant Flash Fiction, Abyss and Apex, Public Poetry, and Lindenwood Review. He writes in multiple genres, publishes space fantasy novels, and dabbles in poetry. He lives in the Dallas area with his wife and rescue dog Gretchen. cjerickfiction.com

Curtis L. Crisler, born and raised in Gary, Indiana, is an award-winning poet with six poetry books, two YA books, and five chapbooks. Creator of the Indiana Chitlin Circuit and the sonastic poetry form, he is Indiana Poet Laureate and Professor of English at Purdue University Fort Wayne. A literacy activist and co-editor of poetry for museum of americana. poetcrisler.com

Debra Wilk is a Chicago native poet, artist, and musician living in Sanford, FL. A retired teacher and arts advocate, she taught poetry, art, and guitar at Lake Mary Montessori. Her poems appear in Revelry, The Ashville Poetry Review, Water Dreams, and others. She received three artist residencies at The Atlantic Center For The Arts with poets Diane DiPrima, Michael Burkard, and Gregory Orr.

Gabrielle Langley is author of Fairy Tale (Sable Books, 2023) and Azaleas on Fire (Sable Books, 2019). Recipient of the Lorene Pouncey Poetry Award, she has worked as a licensed mental health professional for twenty-nine years, including front-line work with senior adults and hospice patients. gabriellelangley.com

Gabrielle Vasquez is a Hispanic American poet exploring emotions and our relationship with the natural world. Drawing inspiration from moments of self-awareness, she encourages readers to reflect on the world as it truly is. For Gabrielle, poetry is the art of living, feeling, and expressing. gabriellev.art

Judith P. Oppenheim goes by JPOetry on paper. JPOetry started writing in 2019, adding poetry to her creative outlets of piano, baking, and quilt collecting. She is an active member of the Friendswood Library Poetry Workshop. inprinthouston.org

Karen Rigby is the author of Fabulosa (JackLeg) and Chinoiserie (Ahsahta). She lives in Arizona. karenrigby.com

Katelyn Brown has been writing sparingly throughout her life. After years away, she is re-exploring this creative aspect and sharing her work with gratitude and hope for resonance.

Kathi Crawford is a Houston-based writer featured in various literary journals. Her chapbook consider the light is available from Finishing Line Press. Connect with her on Instagram or LinkedIn @kathicrawford. kathicrawford.com

Leticia Urieta is a Tejana writer from Austin, TX, and teaching artist with an MFA from Texas State University. Her hybrid collection Las Criaturas (Flowersong Press, 2021) was a finalist for the Sergio Troncoso Award. Her poetry chapbook Offerings to a Tumbled Temple is forthcoming from Purple Ink Press (2025) and dark fiction collection The Remedy is the Disease from Undertaker Books (2026). leticiaaurieta.com

Lynn White lives in north Wales. Her work explores social justice, the boundaries of dream, fantasy, and reality, and the places and people she has known or imagined. She has been nominated for Pushcarts, Best of the Net, and a Rhysling Award. lynnwhitepoetry.blogspot.com

Margaret R. Sáraco is author of Even the Dog Was Quiet and If There Is No Wind (Human Error Publishing). She is a finalist in the Eyelands International Book Awards, winner of the 2025 Ginosko Literary Journal Flash Fiction Contest, and Pushcart nominee. She lives in Portland, Oregon. margaretsaraco.com, Instagram: @mrsaraco

Robin Reagler is author of The Always, Night Is This Anyway, Into The The, Teeth & Teeth, and Dear Red Airplane. Her poems appear in APR, Iowa Review, Ploughshares, and North American Review. She serves as Honors College Director at Houston City College.

Roshni Baig is a bilingual poet from Karachi, Pakistan, composing in Urdu and English since 10th grade. Inspired by Robert Louis Stevenson, Langston Hughes, Maya Angelou, and Chitra Banerjee Divakaruni, their work explores hope amid life's struggles. Currently an Elementary Special Education Teacher at Fort Bend ISD in Houston.

Sandi Stromberg is an editor at The Ekphrastic Review and author of Frogs Don't Sing Red (Kelsay Books, 2023) and Moonlight, Shaken (Kelsay Books, 2026). A four-time Pushcart Prize and two-time Best of the Net nominee, she was juried eleven times in Houston Poetry Fest. She has edited two anthologies: Untameable City: Poems on the Nature of Houston and Echoes of the Cordillera. Her work appears in numerous journals and in Dutch translation.

Sandra Gustin lived and worked internationally for three and a half decades before retiring in Houston. Her work appears in Poetry, AAP's Poem-a-Day, Bellevue Literary Review, and Five Points. She is author of Balloons Beyond Our Borders (Main Street Rag, 2025) and This Treasured View (2015).

Terry Terrific Egharevba is a Nigerian poet and banker drawn to writing as a way of giving voice to silence. His work explores waiting, resilience, and faith through layered metaphors. Find him on Facebook and Instagram.

Zazie Kanwar-Torge (A.K.A Zazie Productions) is a multidisciplinary artist and composer working in avant-garde music, sound art, experimental film, and outsider visual art. He creates immersive, conceptually provocative works that dissolve boundaries between noise, narrative, and the subconscious.

www.ingramcontent.com/pod-product-compliance
Lightning Source LLC
Chambersburg PA
CBHW051325120626
46547CB00015B/2398